Rogue's Galley Proofs

Poems by Mark Matzeder

Kansas City Spartan Press Missouri

Spartan Press
Kansas City, Missouri
spartanpresskc.com

Copyright © Mark Matzeder, 2019
Second Edition
ISBN: 978-1-950380-23-7
LCCN: 2019938174

Design, edits and layout: Jeanette Powers, Jason Ryberg
Cover and interior photos: Mark Matzeder, Bill Peck, Lisa Matzeder
All rights reserved. No part of this publication may be
reproduced or transmitted in any form or by any means,
electronic or mechanical, including photocopying,
recording or by info retrieval system, without prior
written permission from the autho

This book was originally part of the Spartan Press POP Poetry Series, which ran from 2015-2017.

I'd like to acknowledge Pop Poetry, Jeanette Powers, and Jason Ryberg for giving me a voice in this series and diligently formatting the proofs.

-MM

Table of Contents

Scroll of Many Muses / 1

Whistle Stop / 3

Empress of the Winkies / 4

Enchanting / 7

A Front Sweeps Through Lovingston / 8

The Springer Show / 10

Bamboo Poles & Fishing Holes / 12

A Warm Front Sweeps Through Lovingston / 15

Altared / 17

Passions / 18

Legacy / 20

Did Dinosaurs Have Sentience? / 22

Untitled / 24

This is Called Wacamolé / 26

Elegy / 30

The Shrine / 32

Autumn Years / 34

Pillow Talk / 35

Manifest / 36

Book Burning / 39

The ATM at Brookside / 41

The Wall / 44

Monsters / 46

Drums / 47

The question is, said Alice, *whether you can make words mean so many different things.*

The question is, said Humpty Dumpty, *which is to be master.*

—Lewis Carroll

Scroll of Many Muses

Modern wizards weave their spells
in ones and zeroes on glowing handheld tablets,
which I understand is just a different way to do things
and those spells, too, might touch a soul
by what they summon from the world
of pure imagination or the dark and shadowed
corners of some heart,
but I am old school in the arts
and crave the touch of pen in hand
scratching out the several letters of my spell
pouring out to thirsty page
glyphs whose shapes no way convey
the sounds we have ascribed them
by mutual consent, long ages past
yet you, yourself, you know these glyphs
and seeing them you hear the sound
and conjure in your mind their sense

in the beginning was the word
and the word was with god
and the word was god
which word wonders that we crawled from the mire
and taught each other to name objects and acts
which names were spells of summoning or binding
we cast face-to-face or from afar
creating joy or horror, empathy or anger
in the halls of shared humanity
summoning memories deep, dormant, castaway
binding us to each other, to our world, to history

wizards today cast cyber spells of light
emitting diodes with aught and naught
most know not what but as for me
give me vellum and a quill and well of ink
distilled from the blood
of newborn myths and dreams.

Whistle Stop

A train roared through my head last night
with manifests of things undone
and moaned laments of my regrets
and telegraphed the chances missed.
I sat there, still, and heard the steel,
I felt the rumble in my soul
I listened long to loss it left
then exhaled all that might have been.

Empress of the Winkies

We're not in kansas anymore, toto,
she said offhand while looking out
her penthouse view of emerald city,
plush pillows puffed around her
and her little dog, to whom she
addressed droll commentary
with a slow rotation of her right wrist
to punctuate pontification.
Still, while waxing loquacious on goings-on
in theatre, and opera, and art museums, and her
cavalier descriptions of roots gnarled deep beneath
the udc and dar, much deeper than the pilgrims' feet,
to anglican priests and second-sons of minor english lords
who thrust themselves into virginia wilderness
as they would the milkmaid's daughter,
her learnéd discourse sometimes
skips the light distracted, betrayed by words like
git, acrost, or worshington.

There is no place like home, they say,
but home is where the heart is
and the empress' heart is caged so deep within
nick chopper's, not pandora's, chest
it shows no hope of liberation,
sign of restoration,
hint of jubilation. think:
no more hard-scrabble eggs and bacon
served up on drab mismatched dishware
but eggs benedict on a bed of kale
atop royal doulton plates;
not momma's calloused hands smoothing
her gingham apron around her birth-battered body
but the tanned and scented man hands
on back and shoulders, glutes and thighs
the sighs of sage and burbling digital nature sounds,
an anxious time of relaxation.
Buffeting the scarecrow of it could have been
the cousins, friends, and classmates
who stayed stuck in the monochrome great plains
of dorothy gale's sound stage hollywood
that made capote's blood run cold,

the dried out dust bowl steinbeck's okies fled,
the pale, bleak landscape america flies over
on her way from coast to coast.
The empress forgets there's more to life
than penthouse views and city lights.
she forgets those kansas greens and golds, and
reds and yellows and richer azure cloud corrals
than ever could translate to black and white.
Her lionhearted pride of purpose
growling braggadocio rings hollow:
how the mighty—how they've fallen
mene mene, all she wrote.
Somewhere beneath her, emerald streets
encircle some bucolic park here planted
that the teeming masses of the
greatest city in the world
might tread the tracks of the almighty
when morning has broken by dawn's early light.
But the empress in the penthouse
lies with eyes blocked from the sun
preferring neon nights to over-cultured gardens
filled with flowers no one eats
she has seen the real thing and
you can't go home again.

Enchanting

I took a dandelion wand today
and wafted wide a swath of fluff
my spell
fell
like parachutes upon the lawn.
The man who lives there
might think that they're weeds
but I see seeds
vitality
and life.

A Front Sweeps Through Lovingston

I hear ghost cannon
in the valley beyond the ridge
and wonder if stonewall's brigade
have risen from their several graves
and begun to lay barrage
of shells beneath the walnut trees.
It echoes between blue ridge hills
cascading off the wooded rocks
and now a *crack!* like sniper shot
resounds among the trees.
And now the air lies still as death
except that I expect to hear
a rebel yell ring down the slopes
and strike a chord of hidden fear.
Another *crack!* breaks in the sky
a flash of light
a scent of flame
a cloud of gray-clad johnny rebs
sweeps the crest and drives away all blue
that spreads like pickets here about.

And then a wave
disturbs the leaves
like counter-charges down the hill.
The flanks retort
staccato taps
of drummer boys whose cadence rolls
upon the leaves and roofs
and streets and panes.
The town, now drenched in driving rains,
belongs to bobby lee, again,
as years are washed away and left
in puddles on the ground.

The Springer Show

Rob liked white trash cuties:
the sluttier the better, he said.
His wife had a problem with that.
Rob went for biker babes,
and honky-tonk cruisers,
the rock 'n' roll groupies
and greasy-spoon servers.
Carole worked hard
to escape from that world,
kicking a heroin habit
and an even more difficult
appalachian accent
to become a well-respected
middle school teacher
long before she met rob.
So it is a slap in her face
whenever he steps out
to nail some stray
trailer park tramp.

Carole shrieks at him
with that blue ridge twang,
making him a randy statue
for their make-up tryst.
One day she'll take
her old pappy's advice
and pump buckshot into his ass.

Bamboo Poles & Fishing Holes

A leather man and porcelain boy
turn over crusty cow pies.
The boy snatches wriggling worms
from the wet soil beneath.
red ball jets and work boots flatten pasture grasses.
Watch out for snakes, the baritone sings,
then laughs at the falsetto squeals of his daughter's boy
skipping back to his side.
He wraps the boy's hand in his great, grizzled mitt—
brown and cracked as the soil he has worked for long
years—
and leads him to the catfish crick
cutting like an artery across the back forty.
Along the bank, he hollows a nest
in the crook of a live oak's gnarled roots
where a tender sapling stands for protection.
Now vlad tepes to squirming earthworms,
his deft, calloused fingers thread two hooks
through the fat annelids
like Saul the tentmaker threading a needle,
like William Tell singing an arrow through hoops.

He swings the boy's line over the water,
laying the red and white plastic bobber
like a frog's egg on the surface.
His own bamboo pole lodged in a root and rock crevice,
he finds a whittling stick.
The old man shows infinite patience,
more than the boy has with the fish,
as the child lifts his bobber and crashes through the brush
seeking a better vantage.
Bottom-feeders don't care
how much noise he makes.
Eventually one snags the hook.
The boy's bobber plunges, then jumps,
dancing on the surface.
The boy yanks his dinner to its doom.
Watch the spikes, the man says, indicating the catfish's
whiskers.
His experienced hand directs,
wrapping around the small fist, grasping a knife
crunching it through flesh and bone,
then flinging the head for the carrion eaters,
scavenger for scavengers.
Fishtail follows, followed by guts.

With pliers, he shows how to strip skin from flesh,
then runs blade down belly and picks out the spine:
a fine filet for grandmother's griddle;
no dinner ever tasted half as good.

A Warm Front Sweeps Through Lovingston

The sun has set,
the night yet undescended,
the encroaching late spring storm
packs the air with ions,
a green, electric atmosphere
like living in a video.
A huge, black cloud rolls in
over walton's mountain,
enveloping the jigsaw puzzle trees—
the oaks, live oaks, and maples,
the dogwood, spruce, and pine—
enfolding victorian gingerbread homes
like a familiar lover,
engulfing a slice
of norman rockwell pie.
A few cool drops of the approaching rain
mists passersby
like the fringes of a waterfall,
like turning on a garden hose

and spritzing the pistol nozzle
to see the rainbow trapped within.
Now honeysuckle fragrance hangs
heavy as old maid's perfume,
staving off the stench of death.
Now the sky breaks forth with sparks
and cracks like gunshots in the air.
Now the *rat-a-tat* of snare drum raindrops
rolls on the street
and echoes on the roofs.
The lawyer stills his front-porch rocker
and releases his waxed, white handlebar.
He sticks a finger in his paperback
to mark his place
and goes inside.

Altared

Yeah
I said *I'm into bondage.*
but I was thinking more
of wrists and ankles
wrapped in silk;
and not this corporate leash
(hand-picked by you
to match my shirt)
that drags me down
to cubical plantations
where wage-slaves sit
enrapt at lcd altars:
waiting for some
double-breasted overseer
to rip their hearts
from out their breasts
and offer them
atonement to the rodent gods
whose races seem
too great a price to pay
for some small token
of your love.

Passions

I know now how jesus felt
with that cold bitch hovering about
and telling him he was divine
while looking down her princess nose
at the carpenter whose brow
sweats pottage for their bowls.
For this I schlepped to Bethlehem?
she winces at the thought that she
sat astride an ass and thinks
it's still an ass she rides,
that just because this man lacks drive
does not excuse her boy, her pride,
from setting out to carve himself
a name above all names.
It's only for your good, you know,
it's just because I love you so;
and don't you think you could do more
than toil away each day and gather splinters?
Can it be any wonder, then,

that he high-tailed it out of town
and walked about as far as he could go,
down to jerusalem to lose himself in crowds?
And when they came to look for him
he told the crowd he had no kin
and sent them packing back to nazareth.
When in gethsemane he asked
could not this bloody cup be passed
he might have sought his father's face
but heard his mother's voice:
Christ, after all I've done for you—
my joy, my blessed son—
you cannot even bring yourself
to do this thing for me?
on your deathbed, don't cry to me
"I could have set my people free
if only I had listened to my mother!"
but no, you'd rather hang around
head in the air, feet off the ground
and whine that god's abandoned you.

Legacy

Born nine months in cleveland
after some long-haul rig jockey
met a teenage girl still smarting
from a flubbed cheerleader tryout
and too much three-two beer
purloined from a cooler
in the back of brother's bug.
Without a chance—
growing up in grampa's gaze
whose clenched jaw never opened
to speak one word of judgment,
nor yet one of praise
as the cheerleader schlepped blue plates
to an endless rush of drivers
carrying goods from there to here
and back again.
Never once
did the daddy show his face again
though a parade of uniforms
brought momma's bastard home

from where he courted trouble
and lolitas of his own
until he introduced one
with a belly full of him.
Kicked his ass
did the beleaguered great-grampa
with one more mouth to feed
though she embraced them both:
the child her son had sired
and the child who bore this legacy
none of them could shake.
without a chance.

Did Dinosaurs Have Sentience?

Did dinosaurs have sentience?
Did they worry at their kitchen tables
with less money left than month?
Did they hold gofundme efforts
to collect their cousin's bail
just because that bitch he married
told the cops he beat her up?
Did they avert their gaze from *stegosauri*
sitting at the exit ramp
with a swatch of faded cardboard
outlining their sad tale
pleading *please help* to passersby
with arms too short to reach
the pockets where they kept their change
if they even cared to try?
What would they do with sentience?
Would they spend long weeks in mourning
wearing sackcloth & gray ashes
'til a decent time had passed

after velociraptors tore
their sister-in-saur in half;
or when her hapless offspring
suffered such a fate
sniffing down there by the tar pits
where the dino-ruffians roamed
who had got his mother killed?
Were they aware of their own deaths,
these sentient dinosaurs?
Did it alter their behavior?
Did they call in desperate anguish to
some dragon-god to save them
from the problems that they made?
Of the dinosaurs with sentience,
did one watch the rock of god
split the sky and plume the ground
and let loose apocalypse
and did he think the dinosaur for
that can't be good before
returning to the entrails on his plate?

Untitled

The lord g-d almighty
dons his form-fit football jersey
emblazoned with the numeral *1*—
which is an inside joke,
him being the one g-d, and all—
and his team-colors triangle
pennant on a stick
(another inside joke, you know).
He perches on his heavenly throne
wishing he still had a footstool
which used to be in turkey
but the ottomans are gone.
And he calls for mikay-el,
and rafay-el and gavriy-el
(though ari-el is not a fan
of sports and opts instead
for disney films on blu-ray disc).
The seraphim all know enough
to shut their thousand eyes
and cool it with *kadosh kadosh*
until the sports are done.

They watch all games in unison
with no sports channel package
the angels keeping careful watch
to see which teams are blessed.
It's hard to tell, so many teams
give heaven credit for those plays
that were just luck or skill.
But the athletes seem to think they need
to give g-d all the glory
and a thousand thousand fans call out
for a miracle or two.
And, sure, a billion people faint
in some stage of starvation
as famine, pox, and pestilence
are raging through the lands.
And army shoots at army
(though civilians mostly die)
but who expects the holy one—
blessed be his name—
to pay attention to such things
when there are conference games to watch
and touchdowns to be made?

This is Called *Wacamolé*

On expedition to the grocers'
questing after the elusive
pyramid of food they lauded
in lore and on the backs of
cartoon-flavored cereal boxes
when my path looped me through produce
though there was nothing there—
but perchance a peach—
I might have purchased.
My cart dragged me down an aisle
between a hot-house tomato display
and another overflowing
with the wrong species of peach,
then stopped me short within reach of
quetzalcoatl's emerald horde:
a display of luscious avocados
piled from my crotch up to my chest.
I stood and savored that trove of treasure
that pyramid of fruit whose shape

betrays its reproductive role:
seed-bearing ovum of exotic
tropical flora,
each dimpled, ovoid-skin a rich,
deep bluish-green much richer than the hue
some genius called avocado.
though I guess he meant instead
that succulent pulp sandwiched inside
between thick skin and snooker cue-sized seed …
the color of guacamolé. guacamolé.
Wakka wakka wakka.
I make a mean guacamolé.
I love guacamolé.
But—in people's exhibit 6 trillion and something
that life, the universe, or whatever
is not fair!!!—
I developed an allergy to avocados.
So I wasn't going to buy one,
but I could worship them. From afar.
Sort of like the married man
on a tropical beach.
If squeezing specimens were allowed.

When avocados as a fad food
first reached mid-atlantic states—
back in the 1980s, if you're old enough
and still young enough to remember that far back—
and corporate agriculture was trucking them
from texas and california
and stone age truck techniques
meant migrants picked them child-bride early
so the fruit could ripen en route ...
except few did,
leaving a bumper of immature fruit
in all the shades from yellow-green to dark lime
skins both slick and hard as tortuga-shells
protecting all the vague promises within
fruit we set in our kitchen window sills
and watched sit, slowly darkening,
so slowly some would help them
on their way with a short microwave burst ...
which wasn't effective for that purpose
by the way,

    but these ...

these were lolita-ripe—soft but firm—
at just the tender cusp between
too immature to open and
that perfect, luscious, exquisite, succulent,
infinitesimal instant of savoring her perfection.
Their color was rich, greenish blue
bluish-green midnight indigo
almost black enough to fall in headfirst
and the soft give beneath
my fingertips when I squeezed
reminiscent of a lover's yielding buttocks
budged just enough
that our passing ships brush briefly
together.
Like guacamolé.
A sensual pleasure remembered
according to the vagaries of memory—
occasionally with yearning—
polishing the parts too savory to forget,
ignoring parts too bitter to recall.

Elegy

It was good-bye—
she passed his urn,
put her fingers to her lips and
kissed them
carrying it down to
the coffer of ashes and dust
touched her fingers to the lid
so kissed him
one final time
before he boarded the barge.

It was good-bye
to her partner and friend
companion
foundation and crutch
whom she had known
longer than anyone
except her own parents:
classmates and playmates and
one-flesh finishers of each other's
sentences.

It was good-bye
and much too soon
cut short—if not in his prime—
at least still clinging to
illusory vim and vigor
not yet three score and ten
and still too young
to embark on this last cruise
as she wondered
who would finish
her sentences now?
It was good-bye.

The Shrine

The dresser mirror is a shrine
to the one who got away:
with color glossy icons
of all his holy angles
plastered on the glass.
Flanked with a blank verse decalogue—
calligraphied and matted under glass—
his poem to her
and hers to him,
hang left and right
like a pair of sacred scrolls …
scented votives line the base
and a banner of cards inscribed
with hearts and cherubs
is strung across the top.
The idle faces stare out from the glass
looking down
as if from box seats,
or heavenly thrones,

at the wrinkled, linen staging ground
where our bodies merge as one.
Perhaps she's trying to tell him,
look at what you missed.
Perhaps she prays a blessing
of the hornéd god upon his lusty priestess.
Perhaps the audience
incites her praising hymn.
No matter.
I shift a bit
to let the angels see
the rising of the moon
and fill her chalice
with my libation.

Autumn Years

The weather vane
at mrs. p's
is tilted at
an awkward slant
she would have never
countenanced
when she
resided there.
Her new home
is in a home
where people watch her
as she dies
and her proud
but modest home
disintegrates
next door.

Pillow Talk

Life is hard
and if you pick him up
he will just learn
that squeaky wheels
get bathed in grease—
and will squeak ever on
or stand with hand outstretched
panhandling for a free lunch
for him and his date
at my expense—
when we both know
that life is hard
and things get earned
when bathed in sweat
(if even then)
and anything worth having
is worth waiting for
and waiting for
so let him cry
and teach him
life is hard.

Manifest

My grandpa used to hop the trains
and ride them from down joplin way
to denver and the mile high sky
which tasted if not sweet and free
at least less painfully constrained
by ribs cracked from his daddy's fists.

His daddy dwelt down in the dirt
a miner mole who choked on clouds
of dust belched from galena mines
a job well done, a fair exchange,
consideration for the same
before he hacked his lungs into
a pool of whiskey puke.
And so his boy braved icy steel
and bulls the railroads brought to rid
their boxcars of all hobos and their kind.

It was the days of *grapes of wrath*
and dustbowl hobos riding rails
to stand in line for daily work
wherever it was found.
So grandpa wandered for his work
breaking bread to make it last
until the friday crumbs
could trickle to his plate.
He grabbed rungs of roosevelt's new deal
before the rust, when it was steel,
and rode it like a bolt into
a post-war middle class
where all the world was ward and june
and men of steel and plastic spoons
and he could send his children to
the education once beyond his grasp
my grampa hopped a freight today
from where he rested in his grave
and rumbled westward past my gaze
behind the main street crossing gate
as I strolled lazy on my way
checklisting downtown errands.

The arms stretched out to hold back time
letting yesterday roll past
with boxcars' open invitation for a ride.
I stood as close as I could dare
and felt the rush push back my hair
and smelt the burn of steel on steel
while tasting carbon in the air.
He's just like me I heard him say
about that time I ran away
sowing pilfered memories for
adventures of my own
I watched the last car rattle past
then clear a trestled overpass
to leave the taste and smell of all
i have and haven't done admixed
with grampa's rise and fall and hints
of hopes and dreams which he,
his ancestors, and legacy
have heaped upon my shoulders
its whistle blew and moaned beyond
a wooded bend that swallowed the last car
and I looked longingly at emptiness
where promise used to be.

Book Burning

A crewcut child
in short pants and buster browns,
holding granddad's hand,
climbs from the musty interior
of the black '57 chevy
with plastic-covered seats,
climbs a short flight of cement steps
and passes through wooden doors
into the hallowed, book-filled halls
of the baxter springs library.
Awed and overawed
by more volumes, tomes, and books
than ever he imagined in the world,
each page inscribed
with those mystic talking glyphs
of which he is a novitiate.
A spark
by which he sees a million stories
and the sacred well of knowledge

shimmering to slake a thirst
he knows cannot be quenched.
A spark which bursts
in raging flames
with all the fuel piled there in shelves
and he cannot believe
the blessing that is his
that the card in granddad's hand
bestows so freely.
And the boy embraces the flame
which then embraces him.

The ATM at Brookside

Soccer moms in leggings remind me of how I
was supposed to get the house and car and
trophy wife and two point five,
the newest walnut magnavox set prominent
where boys could watch our hometown team
on weekends place or show while I, out on the patio,
grilled up the beast for all the tribe,
popping tops of cold ones and
belly-laughing with joe across-the-hedge
at inconsequential anecdotes
about some blonde big-breasted beauty
stripped playfully of virtue for
the sport of office rakes or warehouse cads
while inside the house the better half
prepared the sides and casseroles
to compliment my bar-b-q
without diminishing its glory
a thousand barbecues before
a gold timex caps years of wilderness

slipped beside the nest egg tucked up
where bough breaks, where crows break in and steal
and lumberjacks clear cut for green
until I slip beneath well-tended lawns
of st. stephen's memorial garden, full stop.

Instead I have this seurat-light
dancing in the leaves
above my head beneath
the prairie's crystal blue cupola
warm breeze bearing canapé tray
of scents from radii of the world
or at least the corner
tucked beneath the shoulder
where kansas waters subjugate
to the big muddy
and dinosaurs' descendants
serenade me from the trees
charlie parker melodies
which art but weren't
and never more shall be

except within the confines
of my jumbled memories
a shadowplay of rippling light
whispering away with zhangzi's butterfly.

The Wall

Because the ones with heart
coagulated in an urban core,
an urban corps, an urban corpse,
we built the walls.
But not the big, beautiful
wall of solar panels
blocking off the drugs
and produce pickers from the South
but thick walls we made of
steel and concrete
singing constant concertina
dc — all fine
along the watchtower
with weapons when we
had to use them
against periodic incursion
of the outliers, the ones
who had no heart but just
a need to hate anything
unlike themselves,

unlike their fathers,
who all of them reflected
their image of some white beard
throne-bound patriarch uranus
thundering down in jealous fury
against all who meet his wrath.
But mostly they're content
to keep to their own kind,
which is what they always
wanted, anyway.

Monsters

Monsters live in the negative space
where leaves caress the sky
where branches thrust into the clouds
like rutting animals in spring
a fecund field of fantastic visions
hovering on the edge of imagination
bursting out in full malignant glory
when shadows lengthen to comport the gloom
enveloping all detail with the
cloak of mystery
then shining its fresnel
onto the mirror of the soul.

Drums>Space>Stella

Remember when we twirled
and your braids unfurled fiery halo
to the corners of the world
and my purple cotton skirt
rose outward like some clockwork parasol
before the flowers you adorned yourself
with lotus petals like the buddha
spun kashyapa's smile
and burst into the dreams of love & death?
Remember when the music danced
with light and telepathic breadth
until the wee hours ran with calliope swirls
when we tasted one another's salt
and weighed the balance to a fault
forgetting all the dreams
of carrots hung on sticks
or brass rings' patina slips
away from all the hope
that clogs the flow of
total sentience.

www.ingramcontent.com/pod-product-compliance
Lightning Source LLC
Chambersburg PA
CBHW030134100526
44591CB00009B/650